MOM,

I wrote a
book about
YOU

Dear mom,

I wrote a book about you. But you helped too. Because it's also a book about the things that we've shared and the years we've spent together, and the memories we've made along the way. All I had to do was collect those favorite moments and write them down here.

And you know what? I think it turned out pretty well. (Probably because I got to write about one of my favorite subjects.) Mom, in my book, you're the best.

Love,
Jennifer

I know it
SOUNDS SILLY
now, but
foR A LONG
TiMe,

I actually THOUGHT you COULD turn ugly if someone said "stop being ugly!"

HEY, MOM!

you may NEVER get me to SAY this out LOUD, but...

it turns out
you were *actually*
RIGHT ABOUT
me not dying if I
actually did
housework. Putting my
hand down the
disposal won't
kill me.

There's a favorite photograph in my mind. It's a Picture of you.

You're here:
on grandma + grandpa's wall

and you're wearing:
your cap + gown

and the year is probably:
1973

and just thinking about it
makes me feel: Like you had
the whole world in front
of you.

Of all the millions of MOTHERS in the World,

You might Be the
ONLY ONE who

Normally doesn't
wrap
presents ha ha

I inherited *your* stubby toes. For real though... your gorgeous looks.

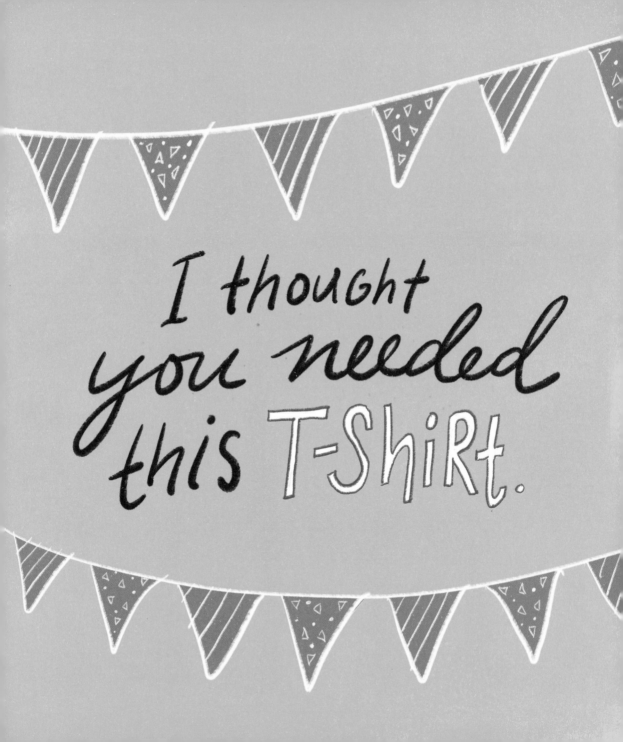

World's most

Likely to be found at casino

MOM

If there's a food that *always* makes me THINK OF YOU, it's

egg rolls OR... meat ball soup

And if there's a SONG that BRINGS BACK a GOOD MEMORY, it's Anything by Kenny Rodgers because you were obsessed with his tape.

And if there's a PLACE IN the WORLD that will ALWAYS BE YOURS, it's

Palmdale

It's pretty much GUARANTEED that future generations in our family will know all about...

YOUR LEGENDARY

Fear of the weather!

"OMG a snowflake just fell."

"clt looks really icy!"

"cl saw a leaf move! clt's so windy!"

"We’re going to be trapped forever!"

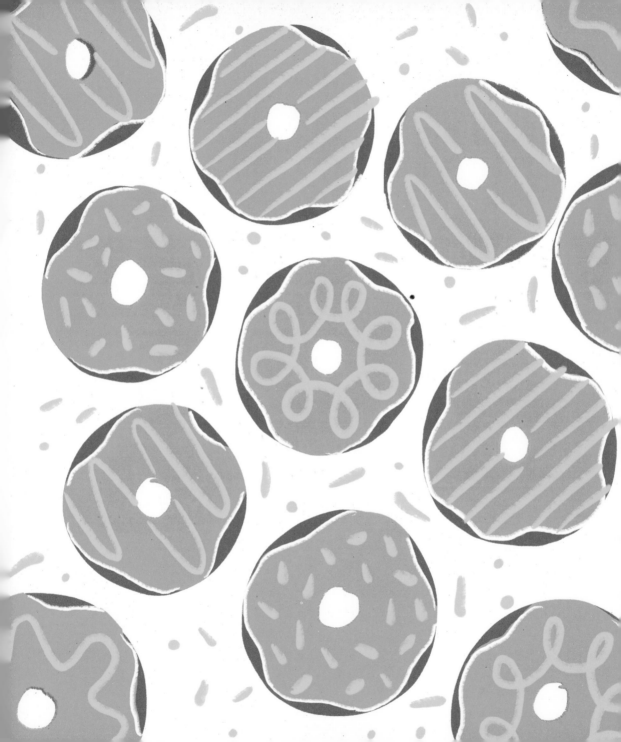

I DON'T KNOW if I ever told you this, BUT I used to think it was the

GREATEST TREAT

IN the WORLD WHEN YOU'D

Take us all to the mall while dad was at work.

You've probably
forgotten
ALL ABOUT
tHiS, But...

oNe of my

fAVORite
MeMORies

is that Time we
went to Semiahmoo +
you kept asking me questions
to things I don't know
the answer to (+ you still do)

Mom - "why do they build the
planes that way?"

"Is this snow going to
melt by
tomorrow?"

If I had to get Scientific about it,

I'd say you're made up of equal parts:
Nurturer
1
Hard worker
2
Good listener
3

I KNOW I didn't appreciate it at the time, But, LOOKING BACK, I'm amazed BY HOW MUCH EFFORT YOU USED to PUT INtO

dressing us so pretty + giving us dog ears.

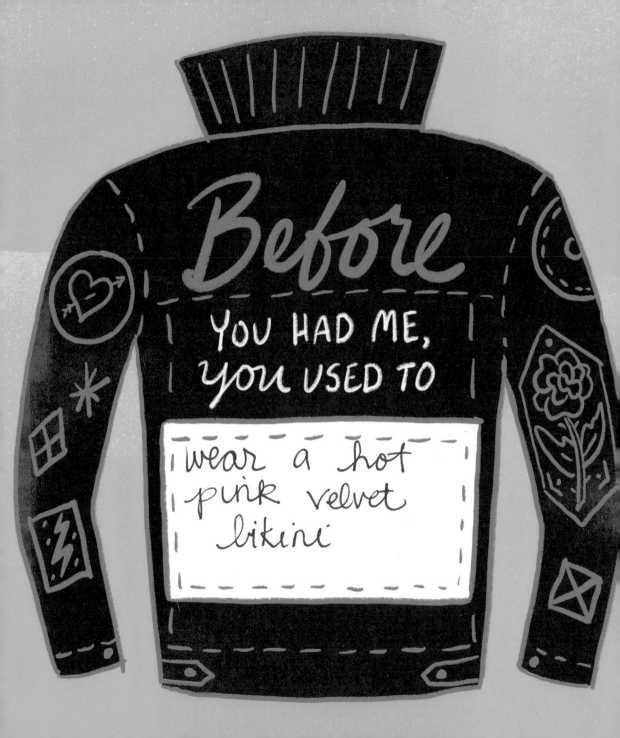

I'm totally certain that THE WHOLE WORLD WOULD Be a better place...

When I WAS LITTLE, I THOUGHT You were a mom who cherished all her children equally.

Now that I'M OLDER, I THINK you are a mom who loves her son the most.

Lee - "leave my mama alone!"

Me - "whatever."

UM, I think YOU PROBABLY DESERVE THIS. →

FOR PUTTING UP WITH MY

bratty attitude when I tease you about your baking ability.

Also thanks for surviving me in my teen years.

EVERYONE I know THINKS it's SO incredible THAT YOU

Have such a gift for design + working with flowers.

AND I have
to admit it:

THEY'RE RIGHT.

I love that the OLDER I GET, the

Closer

OUR RELATIONSHIP becomes.

Just consider this
your personal
HALL of FaMe
WHICH CONTAINS:

Your most
REMARKaBLE
Achievement

Raising 3 kids
+ putting up
with dad.

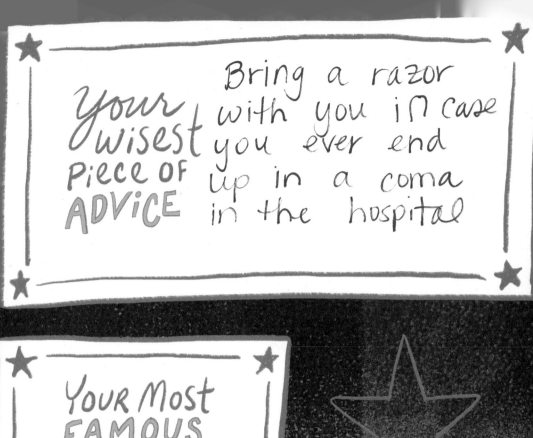

Your wisest piece of advice

Bring a razor with you in case you ever end up in a coma in the hospital

Your most famous saying

Work just sucks

I hope we *never* lose the bond we share.

Whenever
I think about
the time we

Went to CA together +
got an orange charger
+ you said " did
you ask for this?"

I smile.

I realized a
little while
ago that you're
even more
strong
than I knew.

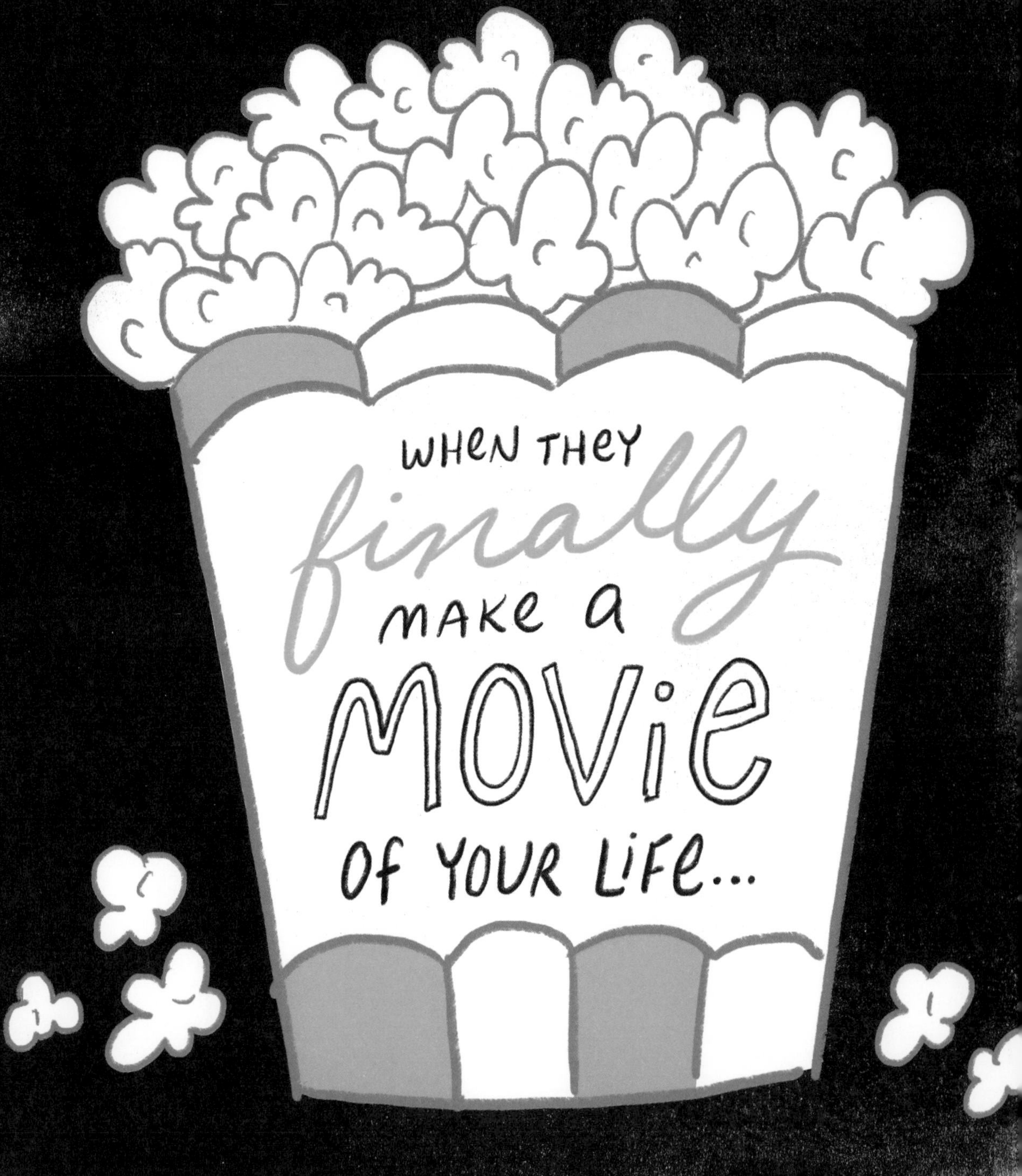
WHEN THEY
finally
MAKE A
MOVIE
OF YOUR LIFE...

HERE'S WHAT IT WILL BE CALLED:

Arleen Mazanek:
   Ultimate Badass

AND HERE'S WHO WILL PLAY the
STARRING ROLE:

Whoever is the most
   beautiful Hollywood
         star

THE SOUND TRACK WILL feature:

All her favorite
         artists

AND the CRITICS WILL SAY:

That deserves an Emmy!

I'm COMPLETELY certain that...

HAVING YOU AS
MY MOM
HAS MADE ME

the cool person
I am today!

If I could
Leave You with just
one thing
to REMEMBER,
always and
FOREVER,
it would Be that...

I could not have made it through my grief without you. You understand me, you let me cry and be mad. You hold me and try to help me to feel better. You were (and still are) there for me in an unconditional capacity. I know you'd do anything to take my sadness away.

COMPENDIUM.
live inspired

Actually
WRITTEN BY:
Jen

WRITTEN BY: M.H. Clark

DESIGNED & ILLUSTRATED BY: Justine Edge

EDITED BY: Ruth Austin

ISBN: 978-1-946873-33-0 | Library of Congress Control Number: 2018941328

5th printing. Printed in China with soy and metallic inks on FSC®-Mix certified paper.

Create meaningful moments with gifts that inspire.

CONNECT WITH US
live-inspired.com | sayhello@compendiuminc.com

   @compendiumliveinspired
#compendiumliveinspired